PLANET ORIGAMI

STEVE AND MEGUMI BIDDLE
Illustrations by Megumi Biddle

BARRON'S

First edition for the United States and Canada published by Barron's Educational Series, Inc., 1998.
First published in Great Britain in 1998 by Red Fox Books, Random House Children's Books, 20 Vauxhall Bridge Road, London SW1V 2SA
Text © Steve and Megumi Biddle 1998, Illustrations © Megumi Biddle 1998, Fold design © Steve and Megumi Biddle 1998
All inquiries should be addressed to: Barron's Educational Series, Inc., 250 Wireless Boulevard, Hauppauge, NY 11788, http://www.barronseduc.com
Library of Congress Catalog Card No. 98-70279 International Standard Book No. 0-7641-0694-5
PRINTED IN HONG KONG   9 8 7 6 5 4

Countdown to Planet Origami

Take a trip from Earth to outer space and back with paper-craft experts Steve and Megumi Biddle. **Planet Origami** shows how, with a little paper-folding know-how, you can make a cosmic collection of stars, spaceships, aliens, and astronauts from just a few simple squares of paper!

Origami Tools and Tips

Make sure your paper is square. (Paper is supplied for you at the back of this book.)

Fold on a flat surface.

Make your folds neat and accurate by creasing them into place with your thumbnail.

Try making the models in the order in which they appear — often the folds and folding procedures are based on previous ones, so you'll find it easier this way.

You'll need: a tube of stick glue, a pencil, a ruler, felt-tip pens, and scissors. (*Always take great care when handling scissors and keep all tools in a safe place, out of the reach of small children.*)

This means turn over the page to continue the model.

This means that the model is complete.

Traditional origami paper is colored on one side and white on the other. In the illustrations the shading represents the colored side. Use **Planet Origami** as a launch pad for your own space-age ideas—try experimenting with different types of paper (wrapping paper, for example) or decorating your models with colored pens. And remember, if you are finding a particular fold tricky, don't give up! Just put the model aside and come back to it another day.

Have fun!

Useful Addresses
If you want to learn more about origami, contact **Origami USA**, 15 West 77th Street, New York NY 10024-5192.

Acknowledgments
We would like to thank Sam Biggs (an alien fanatic) and Hana Kamurahime for their help and support with PLANET ORIGAMI.

Contents

Shooting Star

Try stargazing on a dark and cloudless night, and if you are lucky you might see a shooting star trailing a cloud of sparkling stardust…

You will need:
- STAR: 2 small squares of paper
- STAR TRAIL: 1 large square of paper
- Glue

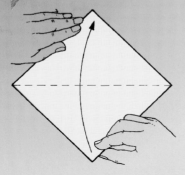

1 STAR: Turn one square around to look like a diamond, with the colored side on top. Fold it in half from bottom to top to make a shape that in origami is called the diaper fold.

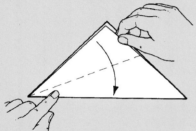

2 From the left-hand point, fold the top sloping side down to meet the bottom edge.

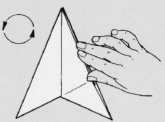

3 Fold the left-hand point behind to the right-hand point.

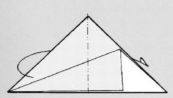

4 Pull the top flap of paper…

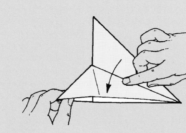

5 …over to the left, so its sloping side meets the bottom edge. Press the paper flat to make a triangular point.

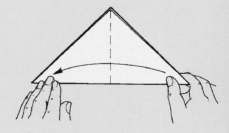

6 Turn the paper around into the position shown.

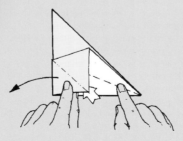

7 Repeat step 1 with the remaining square, but with the white side on top. Fold the diaper fold in half from point to point, making…

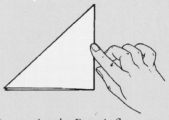

8 …a triangle. Press it flat.

3

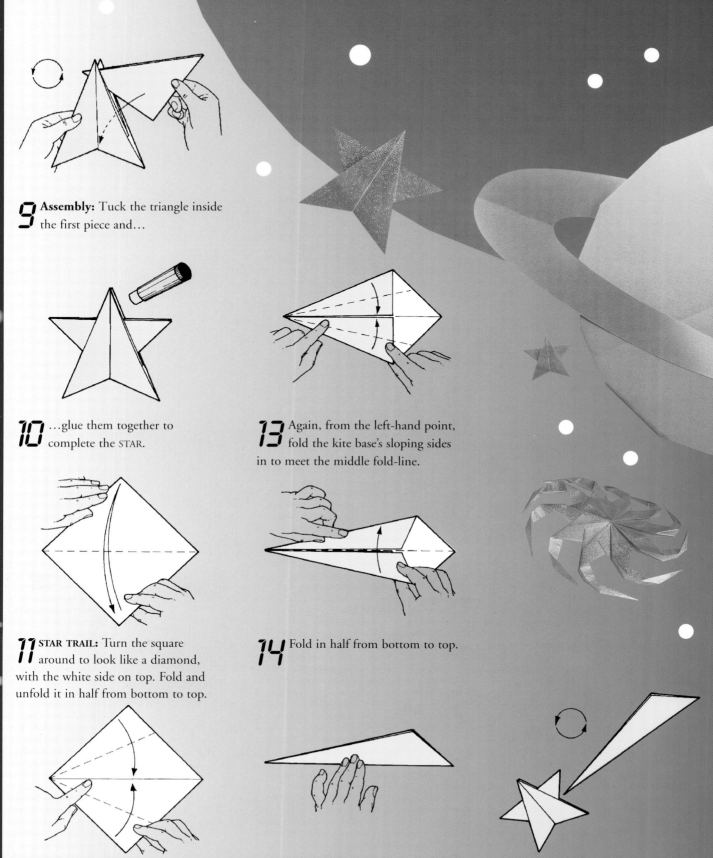

9 **Assembly:** Tuck the triangle inside the first piece and…

10 …glue them together to complete the STAR.

11 STAR TRAIL: Turn the square around to look like a diamond, with the white side on top. Fold and unfold it in half from bottom to top.

12 From the left-hand point, fold the sloping sides in to meet the middle fold-line, making a shape that in origami is called the kite base.

13 Again, from the left-hand point, fold the kite base's sloping sides in to meet the middle fold-line.

14 Fold in half from bottom to top.

15 Press the paper flat, completing the STAR TRAIL.

16 To complete the SHOOTING STAR, arrange the STAR TRAIL and STAR together as shown.

Planet Saturn

The closest planet to the sun is Mercury; then comes Venus, Earth, Mars, Jupiter, Saturn, Uranus, Neptune, and Pluto. Make your own star-spangled solar system using squares of paper in different sizes and colors.

You will need:
- 1 square of paper
- Scissors
- Pencil
- Glue

1 **PLANET:** From the square cut out a square for SATURN and a rectangle for the SATURN'S RING to the sizes shown. Discard the shaded part.

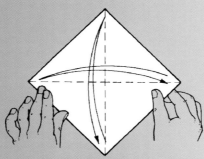

2 Fold and unfold the square's opposite corners together to mark the diagonal fold-lines, with the white side on top, then open up again.

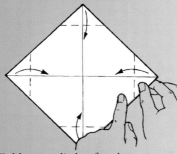

3 Fold over a little of each corner as shown.

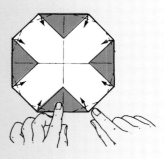

4 Fold over a little of each side point.

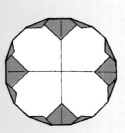

5 This should be the result. Press the paper flat.

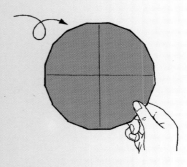

6 Turn the paper over to complete the PLANET.

5

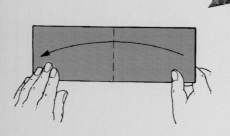

7 SATURN'S RING: Place the rectangle sideways, with the colored side on top. Fold it in half from right to left.

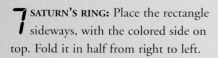

8 Fold in half from bottom to top.

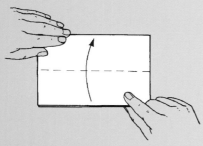

9 Using the pencil, copy this design onto the paper. Cut out the design and discard the shaded parts.

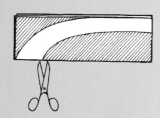

10 Carefully open out the paper into a ring.

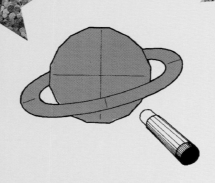

11 Assembly: Insert the planet inside the ring as shown. Glue them together to complete the PLANET SATURN.

Sun

This sun will glow red-hot if you make it from orange and yellow squares of paper.

You will need:
- 8 squares of paper
- Glue

1 Begin by repeating steps 11 and 12 of the SHOOTING STAR on page 4 with each square.

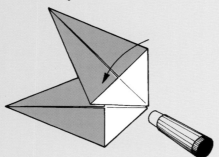

2 Assembly: Place one kite base on top of another as shown. Glue them together.

3 Fold over a little of the vertical edge as shown.

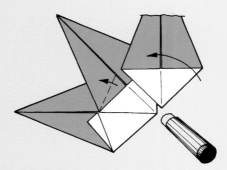

4 Keep on repeating steps 2 and 3 with the remaining six kite bases carefully…

5 … until you have built up the SUN.

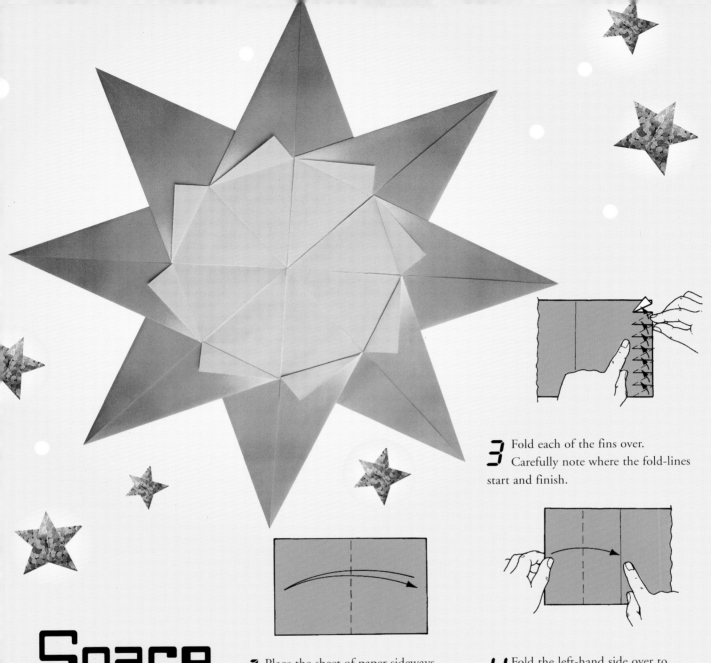

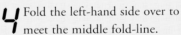

Space Probe

Make your folds neat and accurate, and this speedy space probe will spin as it propels through the solar system.

You will need:
- 1 8½ in. × 11 in. sheet of paper
- Scissors
- Glue

1 Place the sheet of paper sideways. Fold and unfold it in half from right to left.

2 Make seven slits in the right-hand side of the paper, as shown, to make the SPACE PROBE's fins.

3 Fold each of the fins over. Carefully note where the fold-lines start and finish.

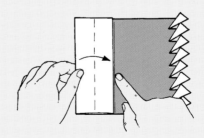

4 Fold the left-hand side over to meet the middle fold-line.

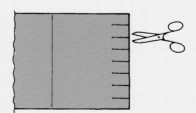

5 Again, fold the left-hand side over to meet the middle fold-line.

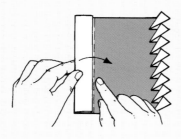

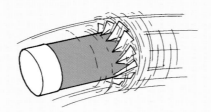

6 Last of all, fold the left-hand side over along the middle fold-line. Press the paper flat.

10 ...and throw it overhand. The SPACE PROBE will glide through the air, spinning around as it goes.

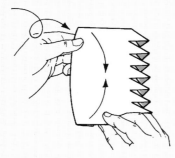

7 Turn the paper over. Bend the paper into a tube, so that the top and bottom edges overlap slightly.

8 Glue the overlapping edges together. Stand the fins up straight to complete the SPACE PROBE.

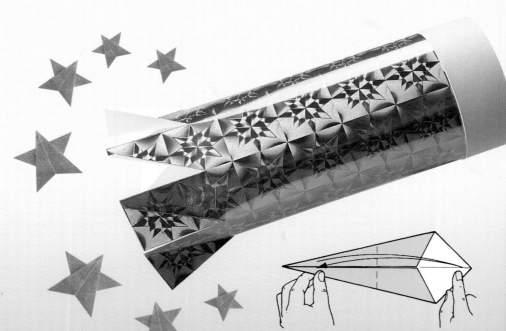

Galaxy

We live in a star-studded system of over a hundred thousand million stars called the Milky Way Galaxy. Create an intergalactic zone with this swirling galaxy model.

You will need:
- 10 squares of paper
- Glue

1 Begin by repeating steps 11 to 13 of the SHOOTING STAR on page 4 with one square. Fold and unfold the left-hand point as shown.

9 Hold the SPACE PROBE near its fins...

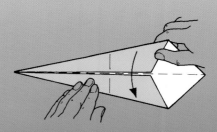

2 Fold in half from top to bottom.

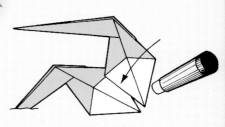

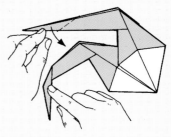

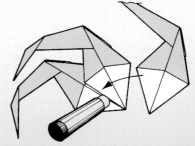

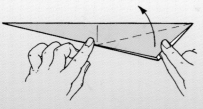

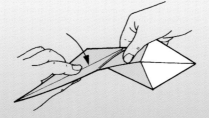

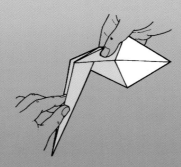

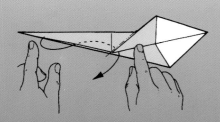

7 **Assembly:** Place one unit on top of another as shown. Glue them together.

8 Fold the unit's tips over at a slight angle.

9 Keep on repeating steps 7 and 8 with the remaining eight units carefully…

3 From the right-hand point, fold the top layer of paper up, as shown to make a flap of paper.

5 This shows step 4 taking place.

4 Now inside reverse fold the left-hand point. Do this by using the flap's sloping side as a guide, and pushing the left-hand point down.

6 Press the paper flat to complete one unit. Repeat steps 1 to 6 with the remaining nine squares.

10 …until you have built up a spiral-like shape. Turn it over to complete the GALAXY.

Crater

The most famous crater on Earth was created 24,000 years ago in the Arizona desert. A 262 feet (80 meters) wide meteorite blasted into the Earth, making a hole 4,150 feet (1,265 meters) wide by 574 feet (175 meters) deep.

You will need:
• 1 square of paper

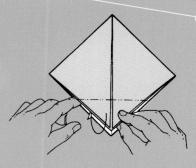

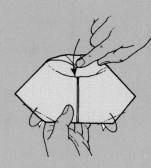

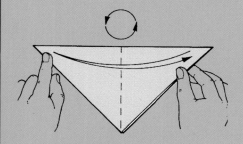

1 Begin by repeating step 1 of the SHOOTING STAR on page 3, but with the white side on top. Turn the diaper fold around as shown. Fold and unfold it in half from point to point.

3 Tuck three bottom points together up inside.

6 ...take on a three-dimensional form as shown. Fold a little of each bottom point up inside to complete...

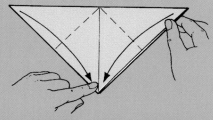

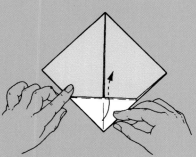

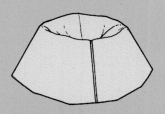

2 Fold the top points down to meet the bottom point.

4 Repeat step 3 with the remaining bottom point.

7 ...the CRATER.

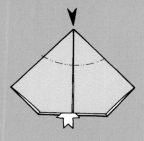

5 Carefully, open out the paper along its bottom edge. Push the top point in, making the paper...

Space Shuttle

The NASA Space Shuttle is as large as an airplane and has a lift off power equal to that of 140 jumbo jets.

You will need:
• 1 square of paper

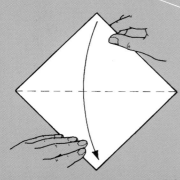

1 Turn the square around to look like a diamond, with the white side on top. Fold it in half from top to bottom, making an upside-down diaper fold.

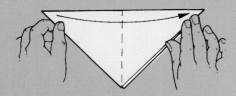

2 Fold the diaper fold in half from left to right.

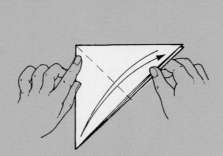

3 Fold the top right-hand points down to meet the bottom left-hand point. Press flat and unfold.

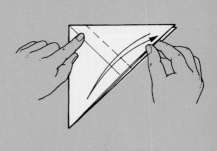

4 Fold and unfold the top right-hand point as shown.

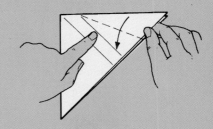

5 Fold the top edge over to lie along the fold-line made in step 4 to make a wing.

6 Fold the remaining right-hand point behind as shown.

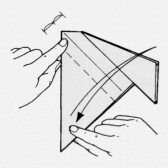

7 Fold and unfold the bottom left-hand point as shown.

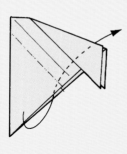

8 By using the fold-lines made in step 7 as a guide, inside reverse fold the bottom left-hand point up inside the model to make the SHUTTLE's tail.

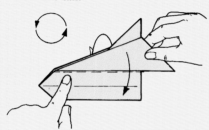

9 Turn the paper around into the position shown. Fold a wing down along the fold-line made in step 4. Repeat behind.

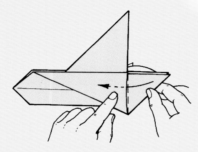

10 Fold the right-hand point over and tuck it into the pocket next to it. Repeat behind.

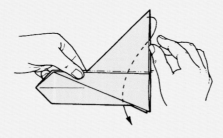

11 Inside reverse fold the tail down inside the model.

12 This should be the result. Press the paper flat.

13 Turn the paper around into the position shown. Blunt the tail's tip with an inside reverse fold. Fold the wings down, so that they are horizontal.

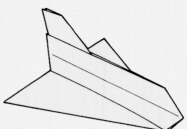

14 Here is the completed SPACE SHUTTLE.

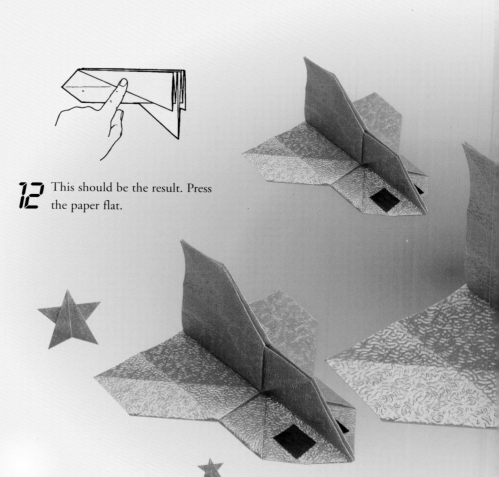

Space Plane

Zip up your spacesuit and zigzag through the universe in this zappy little space plane.

You will need:
- 1 square of paper
- Glue

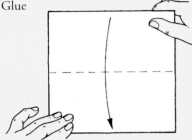

1 Fold the square in half from top to bottom, with the white side on top.

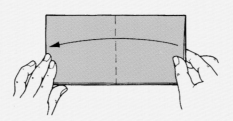

2 Fold in half from right to left.

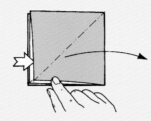

3 Lift the top flap up along the middle fold-line. Start to open out the paper…

4 …and with your free hand press it down…

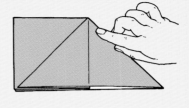

5 …neatly into a triangle.

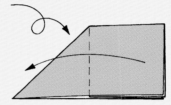

6 Turn the paper over. Repeat steps 2 to 5, making a shape that in origami is called the waterbomb base.

7 Fold the bottom points up to meet the top point.

8 Open out and press the right-hand point…

13

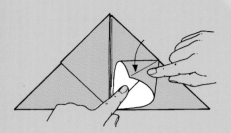

9 …down neatly into a square.

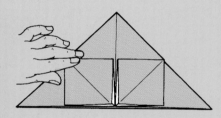

10 Repeat steps 8 and 9 with the left-hand point.

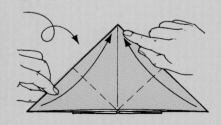

11 This should be the result. Press the paper flat.

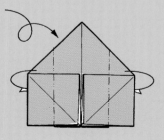

12 Turn the paper over. Repeat steps 7 to 10.

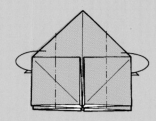

13 Fold the right and left-hand sides behind to meet the middle fold-line.

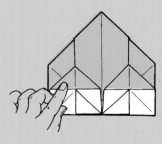

14 Open out and press the right and left-hand layers of paper…

15 …down neatly into triangles.

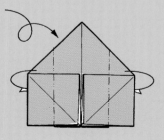

16 Turn the paper over. Repeat steps 13 to 15.

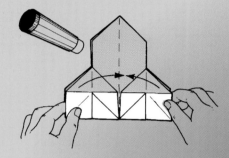

17 Lift the right and left-hand sides up along the middle fold-line. Glue them together, making…

18 …the SPACE PLANE's tail.

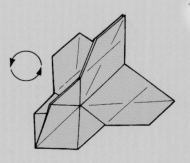

19 Turn the paper around into the position shown to complete the SPACE PLANE.

Launch Pad

Blast off on a journey to infinity and beyond with this launch pad and watch your space plane shoot off into the stratosphere...

You will need:
- **LAUNCH PAD:** 1 square of paper
- **SPACE PLANE:** (See page 13.) Folded from a square of paper one quarter of the size used for the LAUNCH PAD.

WE HAVE

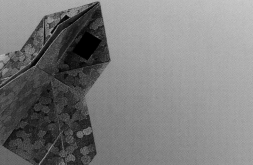

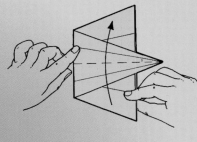

4 Fold in half from bottom to top.

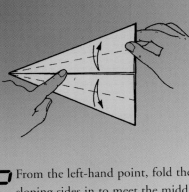

2 From the left-hand point, fold the sloping sides in to meet the middle fold-line. Press flat and unfold.

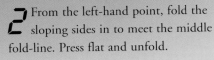

5 Holding the paper as shown, pull up the point that is sticking out...

1 Begin by repeating steps 11 and 12 of the SHOOTING STAR on page 4. Tuck the right-hand point up inside the kite base as shown.

3 Fold the left-hand point over so that it overlaps the right-hand side.

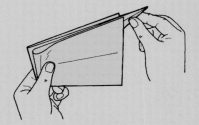

6 ...so that it becomes level with the top layers of paper. Press the paper flat.

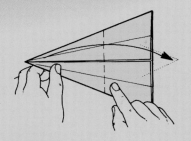

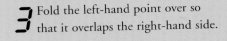

15

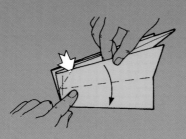

7 Fold the top layer of paper down to meet the bottom edge and at the same time…

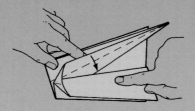

8 …starting from its tip, narrow down the front part of the point.

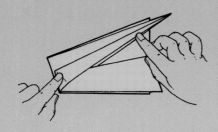

9 This should be the result. Press the paper flat.

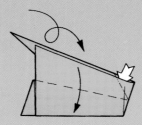

10 Turn the paper over. Repeat steps 7 and 8 to complete the LAUNCH PAD.

11 To work the LAUNCH PAD, place the SPACE PLANE on to the LAUNCH PAD's point. Hold the bottom layers of paper as shown and…

12 …pull them apart. The point will flick forward, shooting the SPACE PLANE up into the air.

Rocket

This fold is based upon the SPACE PLANE. As with all origami models, try changing the angle of the folds, to see how many new shapes you can create.

You will need:
• 1 square of paper

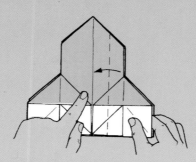

1 Begin by repeating steps 1 to 16 of the SPACE PLANE on pages 13–14. Fold the right-hand side in to meet the middle fold-line as shown.

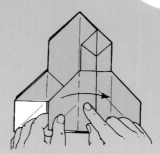

2 Fold the side back out along the middle fold-line, making a fin.

Mother Ship

This is a little more tricky than the previous folds, but with some patience it can be made very easily. Experiment with different colored kite bases—transparent paper looks super-spacey!

You will need:
- 7 squares of paper
- Glue
- Toothpick

3 Repeat steps 1 and 2 with the left-hand side.

5 Turn the paper over. Repeat steps 1 to 3 with the right and left-hand sides.

1 Begin by repeating steps 11 and 12 of the SHOOTING STAR on page 4 with one square. Unfold the kite base as shown.

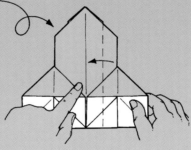

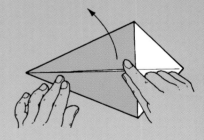

4 This should be the result. Press the paper flat.

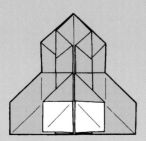

6 Arrange the fins so that they stand out and are opposite each other. This completes the ROCKET.

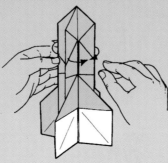

2 From the right-hand point, fold the top sloping side in to meet the middle fold-line.

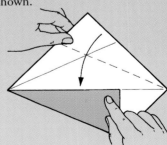

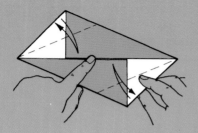

3 From the right and left-hand points, fold and unfold the sloping sides as shown.

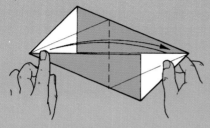

4 Fold and unfold in half from point to point to complete one unit. Repeat steps 1 to 4 with the remaining six squares.

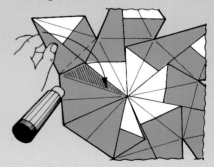

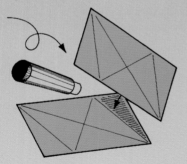

5 **Assembly**: Turn all the units over. Glue one unit onto another, as shown.

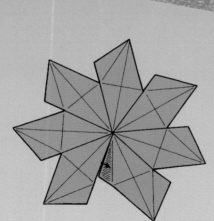

7 Glue the last unit into place as shown, so that the units take on a three-dimensional form.

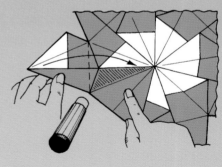

9 ...apply glue to it as shown. Fold the adjoining unit over it, gluing them together.

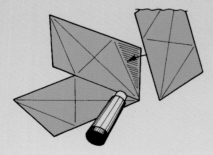

6 Repeat step 5 with the remaining five units.

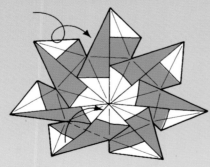

8 Turn the units over. Fold one unit down along the line of the fold-line made in step 4 and...

10 Keep on folding down and gluing the units together as shown...

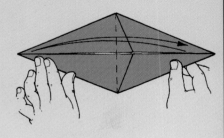

Alien Craft

Make a fleet of alien craft and experience an extraterrestrial encounter.

You will need:
• 1 square of paper

11 …until you have…

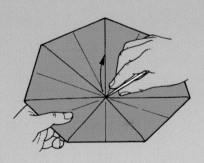

13 By inserting the toothpick into the middle of the dish, carefully pull the top layer apart from…

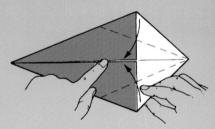

1 Begin by repeating steps 11 and 12 of the SHOOTING STAR on page 4. From the right-hand point, fold the sloping sides in to meet the middle fold-line, making a shape that in origami is called the diamond base.

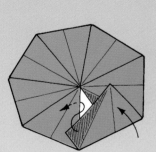

12 …built up a dish-like shape.

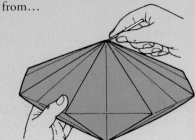

14 …the bottom layer to complete the MOTHER SHIP.

2 Fold and unfold the diamond base in half from point to point.

3 Fold in half from top to bottom.

4 Fold the right-hand point over as shown.

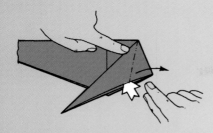

5 Open out the right-hand point and press it down neatly into…

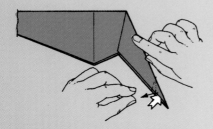

6 …a diamond. Fold the diamond's upper sloping edges behind, making a wing.

7 Open out the wing's tip and press it down neatly into…

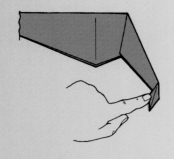

8 …a diamond.

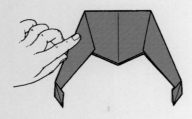

9 Repeat steps 4 to 8 with the left-hand point to complete the ALIEN CRAFT.

Alien

"Is anybody out there?"
Nobody knows if there is life on other planets in the universe…yet.

You will need:
- 3 squares of paper
- Glue

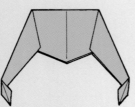

1 Hands: Begin by repeating steps 1 to 9 of the ALIEN CRAFT on pages 19–21 with one square, completing the hands.

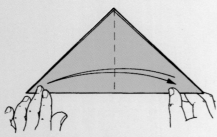

2 Body: Begin by repeating step 1 of the SHOOTING STAR on page 3, using one square with the white side on top. Fold and unfold the diaper fold in half from point to point.

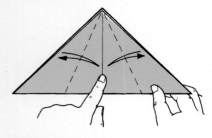

3 From the top point, fold and unfold the sloping sides as shown.

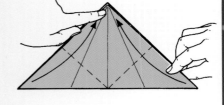

4 Fold the bottom points up to meet the top point.

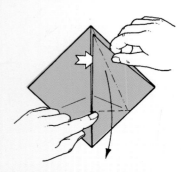

5 Now make a petal fold. Do this by pinching and pulling down the right-hand point.

6 Continue to pull down the point, so…

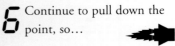

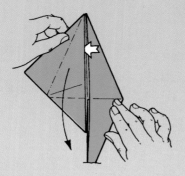

7 …its edge meets the middle. Press the paper flat to complete the petal fold. Repeat steps 5 to 7 with the left-hand point.

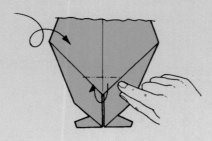

11 Turn the paper over. Fold a little of the middle point behind to complete the body.

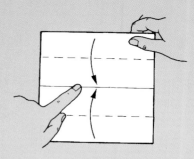

15 Fold the top and bottom edges in to meet the middle fold-line.

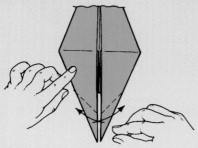

8 Fold the bottom points over to either side, so they cross over each other.

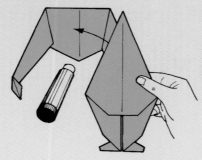

12 Glue the body onto the hands as shown.

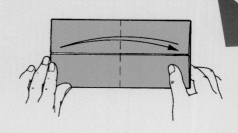

16 Fold and unfold in half from right to left.

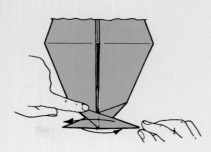

9 Fold the bottom points out as shown.

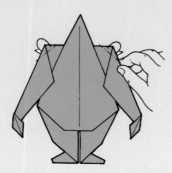

13 Fold a little of the hands' top points behind, shaping the shoulders.

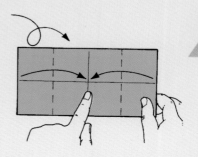

17 Turn the paper over. Fold the sides in to meet the middle fold-line, making four small squares.

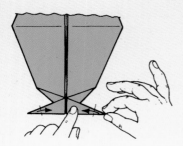

10 Fold a little of each bottom point over to make the ALIEN's feet.

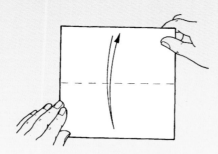

14 **Head:** Fold and unfold the remaining square in half from top to bottom, with the white side on top.

18 Fold the front flap of each bottom small square over as shown.

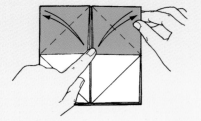

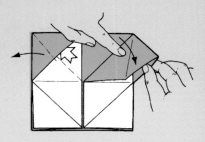

22 …press it down neatly as shown. Repeat steps 21 and 22 with the left-hand pocket.

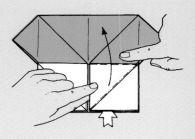

23 Insert your forefinger between the bottom right-hand layers of paper as shown, and pull the top layer up towards…

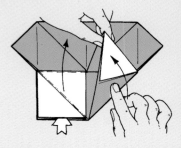

24 …the top edge. Press the paper down neatly into the shape of a triangle. Repeat steps 23 and 24 with the bottom left-hand layers of paper.

20 Using the fold-lines made in step 19 as a guide, fold the front flaps of the top small squares behind themselves, making pockets.

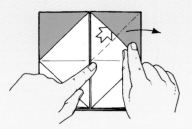

19 Fold and unfold the top points in to meet the middle.

21 Open out the right-hand pocket and…

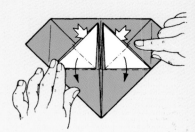

25 Open out the triangles and press them down neatly into diamonds, making the ALIEN's eyes.

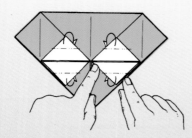

26 Fold a little of the eyes' top and bottom points behind.

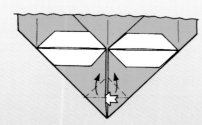

28 Open out the bottom point and...

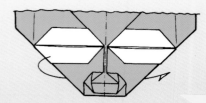

31 Fold the left-hand side behind to meet the right-hand side.

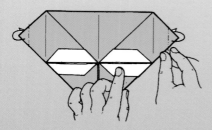

27 Fold a little of each side point behind.

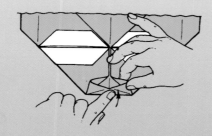

29 ...press it down neatly into a rectangle, making the mouth.

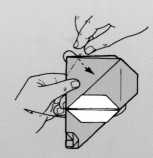

32 Push in a little of the top point to complete the ALIEN's head.

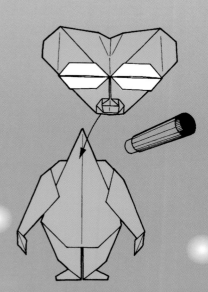

30 Fold the mouth's front layer of paper in half from top to bottom, making two small triangles on either side.

33 **Assembly:** Open out the head slightly and glue it onto the body as shown to complete the ALIEN.

X-Fighter

Space cadets on red alert for the ultimate origami challenge! Follow these step-by-step diagrams closely, and prepare to do battle against alien forces in deep space...

You will need:
• 1 square of paper

1 Begin by repeating step 1 of the SHOOTING STAR on page 3, with the white side on top. Turn the diaper fold around as shown. Fold it in half from right to left.

2 Lift the top half up along the middle fold-line. Open out the paper and...

3 ...press it down neatly into a diamond.

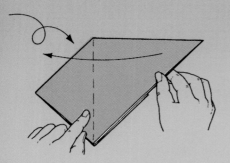

4 Turn the paper over. Repeat steps 2 and 3, making a shape that in origami is called the preliminary fold.

5 Open out the right-hand flap of paper and…

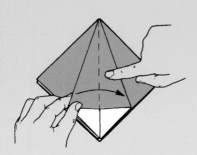

6 …press it down neatly into a diamond. Fold the diamond in half from side to side.

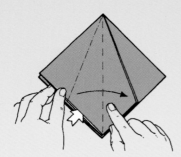

7 Repeat steps 5 and 6 with the left-hand flap of paper.

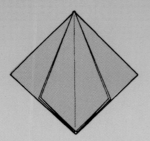

8 This should be the result.

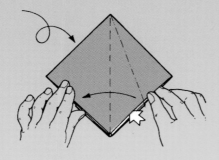

9 Turn the paper over. Repeat steps 5 to 8. Make sure that you have four flaps of paper on each side.

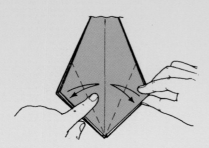

10 From the bottom point, fold and unfold the front flap's lower sloping edges as shown.

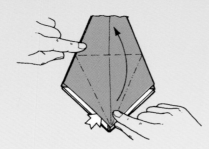

11 Now make a petal fold. Do this by pinching and lifting up the flap's bottom point.

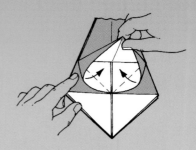

12 Continue to lift up the flap, so its edges meet in the middle.

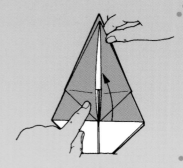

13 Press the paper down neatly, making a triangular flap. Repeat steps 10 to 13 with the remaining three flaps, making a shape that in origami is called the frog base.

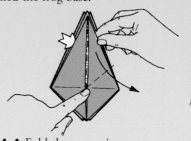

14 Fold the top point over, out to the side and at the same time…

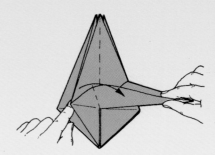

15 …making the adjoining layers of paper rise up.

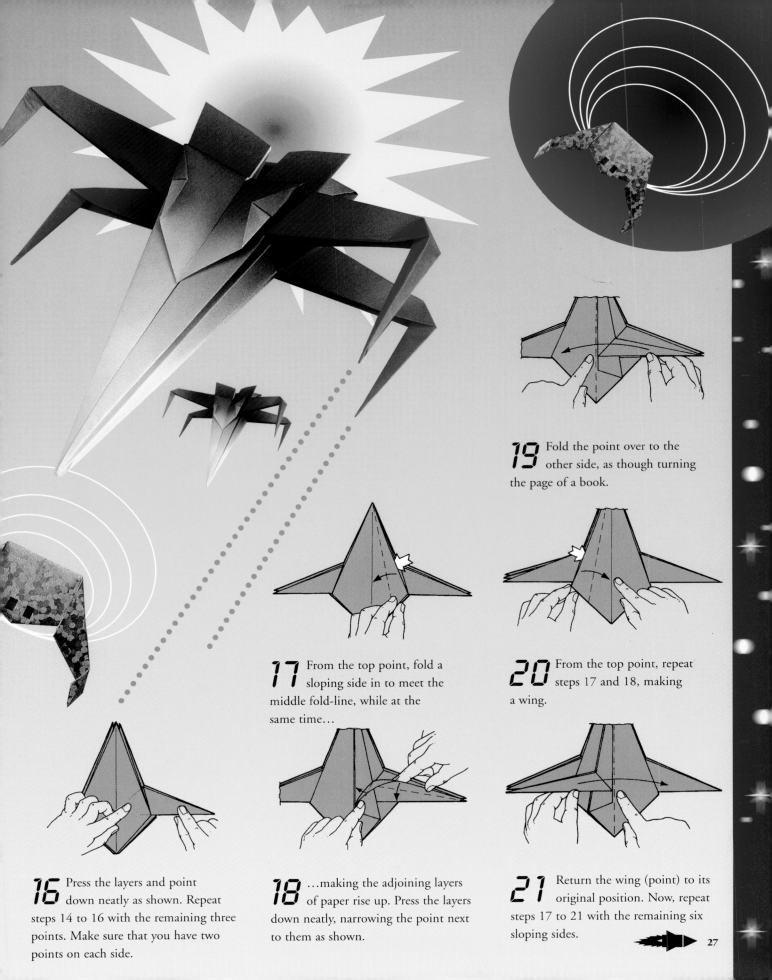

19 Fold the point over to the other side, as though turning the page of a book.

17 From the top point, fold a sloping side in to meet the middle fold-line, while at the same time…

20 From the top point, repeat steps 17 and 18, making a wing.

16 Press the layers and point down neatly as shown. Repeat steps 14 to 16 with the remaining three points. Make sure that you have two points on each side.

18 …making the adjoining layers of paper rise up. Press the layers down neatly, narrowing the point next to them as shown.

21 Return the wing (point) to its original position. Now, repeat steps 17 to 21 with the remaining six sloping sides.

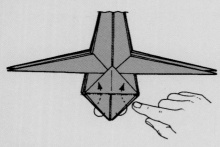

22 This should be the result. Make sure that you have two wings on each side. Fold one bottom point up as far as shown.

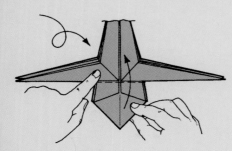

23 Tuck two bottom points up inside.

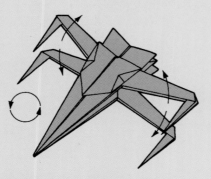

24 Turn the paper over. Fold the remaining bottom point up as far as shown, making a flap.

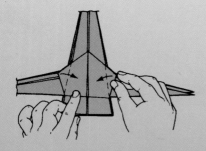

25 Fold a little of the flap's side points in toward the middle.

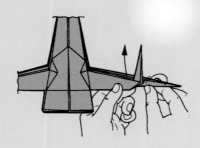

26 Shape a wing with an inside reverse fold.

27 Repeat step 26 with the remaining three wings.

28 Turn the model around as shown. Separate the wings slightly to complete the X-FIGHTER.

Neil Armstrong, command pilot of the Apollo 11 mission, became the first person to set foot on the moon, on July 20, 1969. He was followed out of the lunar module Eagle by Edwin "Buzz" Aldrin.

You will need:
- 4 squares of paper
- Scissors
- Glue
- 1 long thin strip of paper

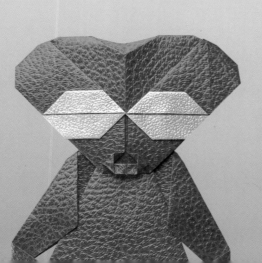

1 Head: From one square, cut out a square for the head to the size shown.

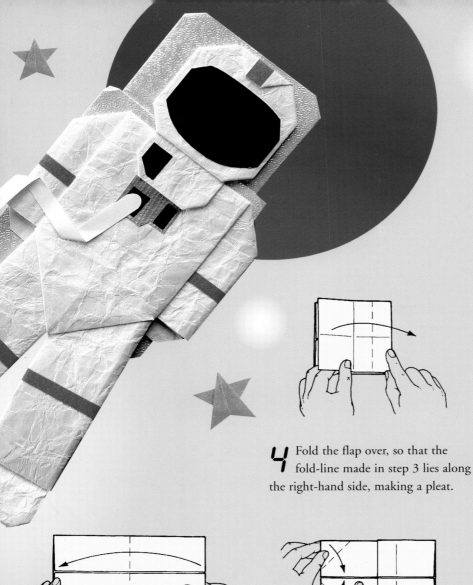

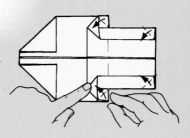

7 ...triangles as shown. Fold over a little of the middle points and right-hand corners.

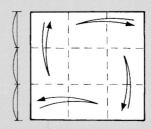

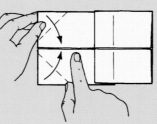

4 Fold the flap over, so that the fold-line made in step 3 lies along the right-hand side, making a pleat.

8 Turn the paper over. Fold down a little of the top edge to complete the head.

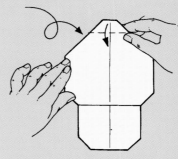

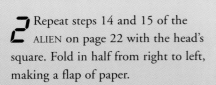

2 Repeat steps 14 and 15 of the ALIEN on page 22 with the head's square. Fold in half from right to left, making a flap of paper.

5 Fold the left-hand corners in toward the middle.

9 **Body:** Fold another square into nine sections as shown, with the white side on top.

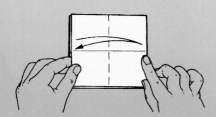

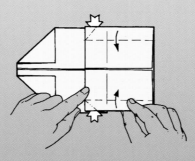

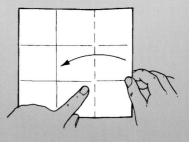

3 Fold and unfold the flap in half from left to right.

6 Fold over a little of the flap's top and bottom edges, while at the same time opening out the upper and lower corners of the pleat. Press the corners down into...

10 Fold the right-hand side over to a point one-third of the way toward the left-hand side.

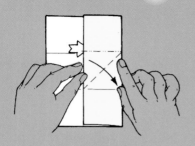

11 Make the folds as shown on the right-hand layer of paper…

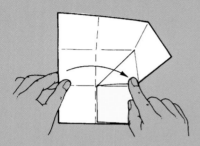

12 …opening it out. Repeat steps 10 to 12 with the left-hand side.

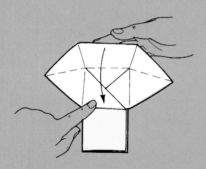

13 Flatten the opened section of paper down into the shape of a roof.

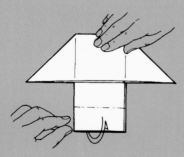

14 Fold the bottom section of paper in half behind. Press it flat and unfold.

15 Make the diagonal fold-lines on the bottom section of paper as shown.

16 Using the fold-lines made in steps 14 and 15 as a guide, bring the bottom section's sides together and…

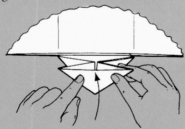

17 …up toward the roof. Press them down neatly into a triangle…

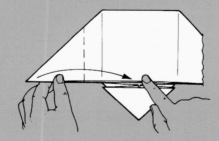

18 …making a waterbomb base. Fold the left-hand point in to meet the middle of the horizontal edge as shown.

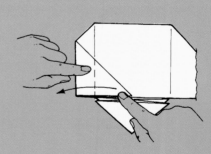

19 Fold the point out along the vertical fold-line nearest to it.

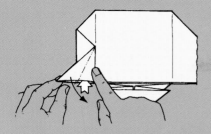

20 Open out the point and press it down neatly into a diamond.

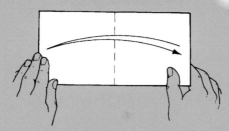

24 Place one rectangle sideways, with the white side on top. Fold and unfold it in half from right to left.

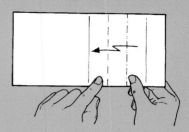

28 Along the fold-lines made in step 26, pleat the right-hand section of paper as shown.

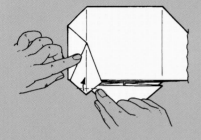

21 Fold up a little of the diamond's tip. Repeat steps 18 to 21 with the right-hand point.

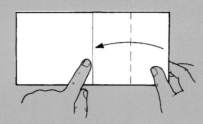

25 Fold the right-hand side in to meet the middle fold-line, making a flap of paper.

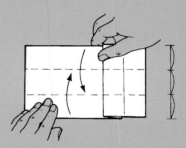

29 Fold the bottom edge up to a point one-third of the way to the top edge. Fold the top edge down so…

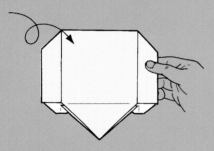

22 Turn the paper over to complete the body.

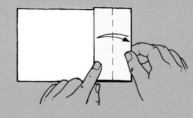

26 Fold and unfold the flap in half from right to left.

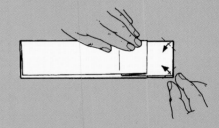

30 …that it lies on top. Fold over a little of the right-hand corners. Repeat steps 24 to 30 with the remaining rectangle.

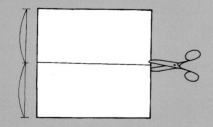

23 **Legs:** Fold and unfold another square in half from bottom to top. Cut along the middle fold-line, making two rectangles.

27 Open out the flap completely.

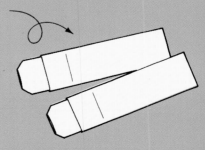

31 Turn each paper over to complete the legs.

32 **Life support system:** Repeat steps 2 to 4 and 6 of the head, with the remaining square.

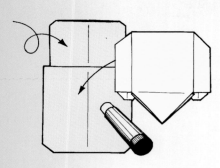

34 **Assembly:** Turn the paper over and around to complete the life support system. Glue the body on to it as shown.

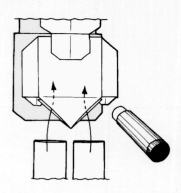

36 Glue the legs into the bottom of the body.

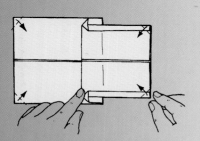

33 Fold over a little of the right and left-hand corners.

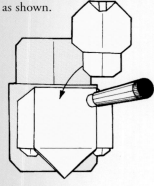

35 Glue the head into place.

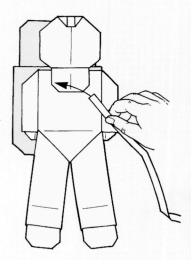

37 Glue the long, thin strip of paper onto the head as shown, making a life support cable. This completes the ASTRONAUT.